W0335799

Fiona
Helbling

Bettina Belitz

Fiona Spiona
A Spooky Bottom

For more of Fiona's adventures in German, read:

Band 1: Falsch gedacht, Herr Katzendieb!
Band 2: Ein Hering mit fiesen Gedanken
Band 3: Ein Popo geistert umher
Band 4: Kapitän Feinripp geht baden

Bettina Belitz

A Spooky Bottom

Translated into English by Ulrike Blank
Illustrations by Alexander Bux

Loewe

FSC
Mix
Produktgruppe aus vorbildlich bewirtschafteten Wäldern und anderen kontrollierten Herkünften
Zert.-Nr. IC-COC-100059
www.fsc.org
© 1996 Forest Stewardship Council

ISBN 978-3-7855-7252-8
1. Auflage 2010
© 2010 Loewe Verlag GmbH, Bindlach
Übersetzt ins Englische von Ulrike Blank
Umschlag- und Innenillustration: Alexander Bux
Umschlaggestaltung: Claudia Lorenz
Printed in Germany (017)

www.loewe-verlag.de

Contents

Holidays with an Ancient Aunt

"Are you feeling alright?" Dad turns around and looks at Zia Zadora worriedly.

"Shall we rest for a while?"

"If you ask me one more time if I'm feeling alright, I will get out of this car and continue on foot!" says Zia Zadora strictly and clicks her tongue. "I'm old, not sick!"

Fiona giggles. Very early this morning the Mammarellas have set out for their holiday in Italy: Mum, Dad, Fiona, her three brothers Fabio, Filippo and Fernando, Great-

Grandaunt Zadora and Beany, their cat. But the best part of this holiday is that this time, Fiona's best friend Leonie is coming with them. It's a bit crowded with so many people on board of Dad's rickety old Volkswagen bus. Every time they drive around a corner, the Mammarellas slide from side to side on their squeaky chairs. Beany does not at all agree with this treatment. Tail tucked in tightly, he is crouching in his wicker basket and meowing so reproachfully from time to time that Fiona laughs out loud. Fabio, Filippo and Fernando are asleep, lying in one big heap on top of each other. A long thread of drool is hanging from Filippo's mouth. Up to a few minutes ago he

was scaring other drivers with his stupid death mask. But now he is tired. Leonie has fallen asleep, too. Her head rests heavily on Fiona's shoulder.

"Just two more corners and we will see the ocean," Zia Zadora whispers.

Excited, Fiona presses her nose against the window. She loves the ocean. And she loves the old Castello in which the Mammarellas are going to spend their summer holiday.

The Castello is an old, run-down castle right next to the beach. It has two towers, an overgrown garden with gnarled olive trees and a large courtyard, where the

Mammarellas have held lots of wonderful summer parties.

The Volkswagen bus turns around a corner. With a grunt Fiona's brothers crash into the door. And Dad already takes the next corner. With another grunt, Fabio, Filippo and Fernando slide to the other side.

"There!" Fiona calls out. "There it is!"

"What?" Fabio mutters sleepily and sits up straight.

"Can't anyone get some sleep around here?" Filippo snaps.

Fernando yawns and rubs his eyes.

"The sea!" Fiona shouts. "There is the sea!"

Leonie is awake now, too, and looks past Fiona out of the window.

Dark blue and glittering, the sea lies before them.

"Oh, how beautiful," Leonie whispers, delighted.

"This is so much more than beautiful, it's superdooperperfect," Fiona beams, "and look, there's the old Castello! We are finally there!"

"About time," Fernando growls. "I think my backside has fallen asleep."

"I rather think it's your brain that's asleep," Fiona replies and dives to the side out of harm's way, so Fernando can't pull her ears.

Zia Zadora hums merrily.

"No wonder that Zia is happy," Fiona thinks. The Castello belongs to Marisa, Zia's best friend, whom she has not seen in a very long time. Fiona has been looking forward to this holiday for weeks, too. Only her brothers have complained.

"Not this stupid Castello again, that's a holiday for an ancient aunt," Fernando has said again and again. "It's so uncool."

Fernando is 16. He would prefer a holiday in a hotel, with a pool, a football field, and a disco.

Fiona thinks hotels are boring. Adventures don't take place in hotels. An old castle at the beach, on the other hand, is made for an adventure.

Quite Ghostly

"Wow, this looks really mysterious," Leonie whispers and looks up at the Castello with big round eyes. "It looks cosy, though, too."

"It is cosy," laughs Fiona. "You'll see for yourself soon."

Sputtering, the fully loaded Mammarella-bus fights its way up to the Castello. Marisa is standing in the courtyard and waving at the Mamarellas with both hands. She is short, very round and wears a brightly coloured fluttering dress with long, wide sleeves.

"Madonna!" she

calls and her voice trembles. “Zia Zadora! Mamma mia!”

With one well-aimed push of her walking stick, Zia Zadora opens the door and gets out of the car.

Marisa throws her arms around her old

friend. Then she hugs Mum, Dad and the children.

“Mreouw,” comes a complaining sound from the back of the car. Marisa flinches.

“Don’t worry,” Fiona says, “that’s only our cat Beany.”

"Madonna," Marisa sighs. "A cat! He scared me."

Marisa's English is not very good, but Fiona likes to listen to her. Marisa's English sounds too funny.

"Beany is very well behaved, he won't do anything," Fiona reassures Marisa. "We only have to make sure he doesn't climb anything; and don't ever let him have white napkins to play with!"

"A cat!" Marisa places a hand over her heart. "Cat sounded like a ghastly."

"Aghastly – what's that?" Filippo mutters confused.

"A ghost, stupid!" Fiona shouts and elbows him. "She means a ghost."

"But, Marisa, surely you don't believe in ghosts, do you?" Zia Zadora asks surprised. Marisa waves both her hands in the air flapping the long sleeves of her colourful dress. "Well, you never knot, Zia, you never knot!" she says and looks up into the sky.

"But now chip chop, to your rooms, unpack your bags. And then we will have a big meals together with pasta and melon and ham and cake."

Her arms outstretched, she waddles off to the Castello's big entrance hall.

"Sounds good to me," says Fiona and grabs Beany's wicker basket.

"Chip chop!" Fernando apes Marisa. "Chip chop to your rooms to the aghastly."

"It's a good thing I don't have to share a room with you. I prefer five ghosts to three idiots," Fiona says decidedly. "Come on, Leonie."

The two girls are lucky: they get a big room all to themselves. From their window they can look down to the beach and the sea. Fiona puts down Beany's wicker basket and opens the latch. But Beany remains sitting inside. Sullenly he stares at Fiona.

"Oh great, now Monsieur is offended," Fiona moans. "Now come on, Beany, don't make such a fuss!"

Slowly, very slowly,

Beany crawls out of the basket. Then he deliberately turns his back on Fiona and begins licking himself thoroughly.

"No idea how this creature can scare someone," Fiona wonders. "As he is himself a scaredy-cat of the very worst kind."

"Maybe Marisa is afraid of all cats," Leonie says, while she is bouncing up and down on the big, soft bed.

"Impossible!" Fiona shouts. "Marisa is Italian. All Italians love cats!"

Fiona sits down on the bed next to Leonie and looks at her questioningly. "So, how do you like it here?"

"Well," Leonie says softly and looks

around. “An old little castle like this is a bit spooky, don’t you think?”

Fiona laughs mischievously. “Maybe a bit. But I like it.”

“Hmm.” Leonie sounds unconvinced.

“Don’t worry, Leonie,” Fiona calms her friend. “We have been here on holiday many times, and we have never ever come across a ghost, I swear.”

“Sure?”

“Sure,” Fiona affirms. “Only if Marisa creeps through the kitchen in her garish green bathrobe, you might mistake her for a ghost …”

Now Leonie is laughing, too.

“This will be the best holiday ever,” Fiona beams. “I promise. Extra-big Italy-promise!”

Ernesto Is Around

“Children! Meals is ready,” Marisa calls from the entrance hall.

“Wow, I’m so hungry!” Fiona says. “What about you?”

“Absolutely,” Leonie replies happily.

Fiona jumps off the bed and opens the door.

“Children! Spaghetti! Melon! Cake!” Marisa’s voice booms through the Castello.

“And one aghastly,” Filippo roars and runs past Fiona and Leonie, the skull mask on his face. Fabio and Fernando follow him, grinning.

“No, Filippo, leave Marisa alone,” Fiona tries to stop him and sprints off after her brothers. She manages to trip up Fabio, and pinches Fernando’s bottom; but Filippo is already down in the entrance hall. Howling eerily, he staggers towards Marisa, who’s just about to light the candles on the table.

“Whoohooooohooooo! Whoohooooohooooo! Maaaariiiiiisaaaa!”

“Madonna!” Marisa shrieks and drops the matches. “Ernesto! No, Ernesto!”

"Eh what?" Filippo grunts and lifts the mask off his face. "Ernesto? Marisa, it's only me, Filippo!"

Suddenly Dad, Mum and Zia are standing in the entrance hall.

"What happened here? Fabio, Filippo, Fernando!" Dad bellows. "What did you do to her?"

"Ernesto," Marisa moans. Her whole body is shaking.

And now Fiona realises where she knows the name Ernesto from. Ernesto was Marisa's husband. And he has been dead for more than twenty years!

"I know you're missing your Ernesto, but we're here now, with you," Zia Zadora says.

Consolingly she pats Marisa's shoulders.

"No, you don't understand!" Marisa shouts and raises her chubby arms. "Ernesto's aghastly is here!" she whispers. "Every night, Ernesto's aghastly is here in the castle."

Leonie flinches and quickly takes Fiona's hand.

"You think this place is haunted?" Dad asks slowly.

"Yes," Marisa replies so softly that Fiona can hardly hear her. "The aghastly of Ernesto goes around."

Leonie shudders. Fiona looks curiously at Marisa.

"And for how long has this been going on?" Mum asks.

"Only for twos or three weekse," Marisa says and fans herself with a napkin.

Beany gallops down the stairs heading directly for the napkin, but Fiona can stop him just in time.

Marisa heaves a deep sigh. "I'm thinking about selling the castlo," she proclaims sadly. "It's much too big for a lonely old woman like me. Don't want to live with aghastly."

"Oh no, Marisa, please don't!" Fiona protests stamping her foot. "It's our castle! We always come here on holiday. You can't Marisa, it's impossible."

"It's her Castello, not ours, Fiona," Dad says sternly. "We cannot tell Marisa where she is supposed to live. And now let's eat."

"Yes, eat!" Fabio pipes up.

Fiona puts down Beany again. In one big leap he's on the table, grabs a napkin and runs outside into the courtyard. Fiona watches him sadly. Beany likes being in the

Castello. All Mammarellas do. And nothing is going to change that. Never ever!

"Marisa mustn't sell the Castello," Fiona hisses at Leonie. "We have to do something to prevent it."

"Oh Fiona," Leonie sighs. "You and your adventures!"

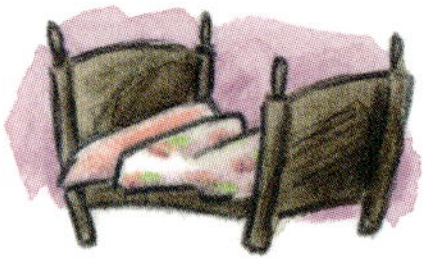

Is Marisa Crazy?

"Fiona?" Leonie murmurs fearfully.

"Hm? What?" Fiona asks sleepily.

She has eaten so much pasta and cake that she's now lying in bed, full and sleepy. It's completely dark in the room. A warm breeze comes in through the window. The sea is roaring outside.

"I think there's somebody here. I heard something."

Fiona sits up straight, yawning. Leonie's blanket rustles.

"There's nothing, Leonie, I'm sure. There are no ghosts here. It's probably only Beany."

"And what if there really is a ghost?"

Leonie whispers. "What if Marisa is right and the Castello is haunted?"

"It's not. And even if it were, that wouldn't be such a drama," Fiona says, yawning once more.

"Why wouldn't that be a drama?" Leonie's voice is trembling.

"Because I've seen a photo of Ernesto. He was a tiny man, as small as Marisa, and not a single hair on his head. I don't think a ghost like that is dangerous." Fiona stretches out her hand and switches on the bedside lamp. Leonie is crouching on her bed, her chin resting on her knees, the blanket drawn around her shoulders. Beany sits on the window sill, the tip of his tail twitching. His green eyes are glowing.

"You see? It's only Beany."

"Alright, but if there are no ghosts – is Marisa crazy?" Leonie asks. Fiona takes a moment to think. "Well, she's a bit confused, sometimes. But crazy – no, I don't think so. What do you think?"

Leonie shrugs. "I don't know. I'm just wondering what it is she hears at night."

"And I'm planning to find out. But not tonight. And tomorrow we'll go swimming." Fiona's eyelids are drooping.

"Fiona?"

“Hmmmm?” Fiona grunts sleepily.

“Can I come over and sleep in your bed?”

“Sure,” Fiona murmurs.

Quickly Leonie crawls over and into her friend’s bed and snuggles up beside her. Beany rolls up into a black furry ball at the foot of the bed. And with the ocean roaring outside and the crickets singing, Fiona and Leonie peacefully fall asleep.

What a Crawler!

"Children, children, isn't that not a most wonderfully day?" Marisa beams at them as Fiona and Leonie come down for breakfast into the entrance hall the next morning.

"Well, somebody is in a good mood!" Fiona grins.

Marisa smiles. "I'm no longer afraid of the aghastly!"

"You're not?" Leonie asks hopefully. "He did not turn up again?"

Marisa pours the girls hot chocolate. "Oh, but yes," she moans. "Was there again, the aghastly. But just now a man has called and told me he wants to buy the castlo."

"What?" Fiona cries, horrified. "So quickly? What man?"

Marisa smiles dreamily. "Signore Bottomi is the papa of a one big family. He has seven children! Ernesto always wanted to have lots of children here in the Castello. Maybe Ernesto's aghastly will be quiet when they are here."

"And what about us?" Fiona asks, her hands on her hips.

"Oh, we'll find a solution, we sure will!" Marisa says. She pats Fiona's tousled hair. "I'll talk to Signore Bottomi. Castlo is big enough; surely there'll always be room for Mamarella children."

"But I don't want to come on holiday to

Signore Bottom," Fiona complains. "We want to be on holiday with you here in the Castello, only with you."

Suddenly, they hear steps outside. A grey-haired man in a pinstripe suit, with golden glasses and a golden watch enters the hall. A fat black-haired boy follows him, throwing Fiona a look as if he had just bitten into a sour lemon. The man opens his mouth into a wide grin. Three gold teeth flash in his mouth.

"I think that's will be him," Marisa says cheerfully and waddles up to him. "Signore Bottomi!"

"Signora Marisa!" The man calls out with exaggerated friendliness. He bows so deeply that his grey hair almost touches the floor.

And then Marisa and Signore Bottomi start talking in fast Italian. The fat boy remains standing next to them.

"So this is Mr. Bottom," Fiona grumbles. "What a crawler. I'll never ever go on holiday with him. Just look at his son ..."

"Do you understand what they are

saying?" Leonie asks Fiona quietly. "You do speak a bit of Italian, don't you?"

Fiona shrugs helplessly. "I understand hardly anything. They are talking too fast."

Now Marisa takes the man and his son to the kitchen. Signore Bottomi pulls a few

sheets of paper from his briefcase.

"I don't believe it! I think they're already talking about a contract," Fiona whispers. "We have to stop them!"

"But how?" Leonie asks. "Marisa is certain the castle is haunted. She does not want to stay here."

"Nonsense. There is no ghost here in the castle! I don't like this Bottom-person. And I like his son even less! *Hick*." Fiona is so angry that she gets the hiccups. She gets up and walks over to the kitchen.

Marisa is busy searching through her drawers. The papers are lying on the kitchen table. Signore Bottomi is standing next to the window, looking outside and gleefully rubbing his hands. His son throws Fiona another dark look.

"*Hick*," goes Fiona.

Marisa turns around. "Oh child, do you get the hickyups?"

"Hmm, *hick*," Fiona nods. "What are you looking for, Marisa?"

"A pen for the signaturies." Marisa beams and continues to rummage through the drawers.

"Oh no," Fiona thinks desperately. "She's really about to sign the contract. What am I going to do now?"

But before Fiona can come up with a good idea, words are buzzing through her mind. Words that are not hers. The thoughts of someone else! Fiona forces herself to continue breathing normally. She is, by now, used to this strange feeling. Ever since her tenth birthday, it has happened now and again that she can hear other people's thoughts. Most of the time, it's when she's very upset – and has the hiccups.

"It's a very special Mammarella gift," Zia Zadora explained. "You'll have to be very careful with it."

Just too bad that all Fiona hears when she's mind reading are bits and pieces of a sentence. Even worse, if these bits and pieces are in Italian ...!

"Otel" and "ricco"; these two little words are all Fiona has heard so far; even though Signore Bottomi hasn't said anything and is still standing at the window, rubbing his hands.

Fiona thinks hard. What does "ricco" mean? Could that perhaps be the name of the boy?

"Ricco," Fiona repeats, lost in her thoughts.

Signore Bottomi pulls away from the window and looks at Fiona in amazement.

Oops! Fiona bites her tongue. Has she said that out loud?

It's a good thing that at that precise moment Signore Bottomi is distracted by Marisa.

"Aaah, look, here I have found a one pen!" she says happily, and with the pen in her hand waddles back to the table.

"No, Marisa, please don't! Please, not now!" Fiona runs toward Marisa and tries to take the pen from her. "*Hick!*"

"But child, what is the matter?"

"Please, don't sign that," begs Fiona.

Signore Bottomi stops smiling.

"You should let … eh, *hick*, you should let

Dad read the contract first. Dad knows a lot about contracts. Please!" Fiona beseeches Marisa.

Leonie and Zia enter the kitchen now, too.

"Just trust the girl, Marisa," says Zia. "Think about it for a while, sleep on it, wait until tomorrow. That's what you should always do with difficult decisions."

"Exactly," Fiona affirms. "Wait one more night. Just one night!"

Marisa drops the pen, looking confused. She does not sign the contract. Relieved, Fiona sighs. But at once there are new thoughts of Signore Bottomi's in her head; and her ears are prickling. The words she is hearing sound evil and mean: “notte” and “spirito”.

Fiona takes Leonie’s hand and pulls her outside.

“Quick,” Fiona cries as they are running through the garden down to the beach. “We have to solve a mystery.”

Bottomi Wants to Be Rich

"'Otel', 'ricco', 'notte' and 'spirito'. Can you remember that?" Fiona asks.

Leonie nods. "Are these someone else's thoughts?"

"Yes, they are, and they belong to this stupid Bottom," Fiona sighs and dips her toe into the waves.

Except for Zia Zadora, Leonie is the only person who knows that Fiona can sometimes hear thoughts.

"Alright. 'Otel', that's got to be 'hotel' right?" Leonie muses.

"Yes, ok, but it doesn't make any sense. This is an old, run-down Castello, and no hotel!" Fiona interjects.

"That's right", Leonie agrees. "But on the other hand ..." Leonie screws up her face in concentration and rubs her nose.

"On the other hand, what?" Fiona asks curiously. Whenever Leonie looks as serious as she does now, she's almost always on the right track.

"They could tear down the castle and build a hotel in its place. Directly at the beach."

"But Marisa has said herself that this Bottom-person has seven children and wants to move in here with his family."

"Wait a minute ...," Leonie broods. "What if he lied and doesn't want to move in here himself? Maybe this was just a trick?"

Fiona slaps her hand against her forehead. "Oh, but sure! You're right! He is no father of a large family; he's just another agent, who wants to make money with the Castello. He wants to tear down everything, the stupid Bottom!"

"That's a strange coincidence, don't you think?" Leonie wonders. "Marisa thinks about selling the Castello, and bang, here comes this Bottomi-person knocking at her door. Makes me wonder ..."

"Okay, okay," Fiona says and dips her feet into the cool water. "We have to keep on thinking. Hotel is clear, and 'ricco'? Could that mean 'rich'? – He wants to become rich with a hotel. So far so easy to understand."

"Alright, but what do 'notte' and 'spirito' mean?"

"Wait a minute, 'spirito'! In sanctus spiritus! They say that in church," Fiona shouts. "That's the Holy Ghost! The Aghastly! Bottom is the ghost! And 'notte' means 'at night', I think. Zia sometimes says 'Buona notte' when I go to bed."

Leonie stares at Fiona with big round eyes. "So this Bottomi scares Marisa at night with spooky noises, so that she will leave the castle and sell it."

"Exactly!" nods Fiona. "This Bottom person really is an evil, shifty crawler."

"And what do we do now?" Leonie asks.

Fiona's grin broadens. Then she drops backward into the cool water.

"That's absolutely clear," she laughs and pulls at Leonie's ankle until her friend falls over into the water, too. "We'll make sure that the aghastly Bottom has a visitor tonight. And we'll set a trap for him."

A Mask, a Cat, a Plan

"All clear?" Fiona asks. "What are the idiots up to?"

Leonie leans far out of the castle corridor's window and looks down.

"They are playing football on the beach," she replies.

"Sure, what else could they be doing?" Fiona rolls her eyes. "They never think of anything else besides football, do they. But please tell me, at once, when they stop and come back up here, alright?"

"Sure," Leonie replies and continues to look out of the window.

Fiona opens the door to her brothers' room.

"Phew, what a mess!" she sighs. Clothes, football magazines, crisp bags and coke bottles are scattered across the floor. How is she supposed to find the mask here?

But then Fiona's gaze drops on Fabio's bed. Something black is just visible under the pillow.

"I think I've got it," Fiona hisses and pulls at the black corner. And indeed: it's Filippo's skull mask!

"Bingo," Fiona mutters happily. She wades through the piles of clothes, back to the corridor and closes the door.

"That was fast," Leonie says cheerfully. "All we need now is Beany."

"And that's not going to be a problem," Fiona reassures her. "I've nicked a can of tuna from Marisa's pantry. We are all set. Shortly before midnight we will sneak down to the courtyard, lay down the clothes line, lure Beany to us with the tuna, tie the death mask to his back, and …"

"… we need a napkin!" Leonie shouts.

"Already got it," Fiona replies and pulls a couple of white napkins from her pocket. "And the Aghastly for Signore Bottom is ready!"

"And you think we will be able to pull all this off?" Leonie says doubtfully.

"Hey, it's going to be

a lot of fun. I told you, these are going to be the best holidays ever," Fiona replies happily. "And now let's go for a swim and annoy my idiot brothers!"

The two friends remain at the beach until a red sun sinks down into the sea, and Marisa calls them for dinner. She serves

them lots of spaghetti with tomato sauce and her homemade tiramisu for dessert. Delicious!

But soon, everybody is tired from the swimming and the hot Italian sun. So at ten o' clock, the Mammarellas and Marisa are in their beds and sound asleep. Only Fiona and Leonie are bouncing nervously on their beds. Frequently, they are checking the clock.

“Ok, only 20 minutes until midnight. We should get going to the courtyard,” Fiona whispers finally. “The Bottoms will surely arrive soon.”

“By the way, have you seen Beany?” Leonie asks.

Fiona shakes her head. “No. He’s probably sitting in an olive tree and doesn’t know how to get down again.”

“But olive trees aren’t that high, are they?” Leonie wonders.

“They aren’t. But sometimes, Beany isn’t

the brightest," Fiona sighs. "In the worst case we'll have to make do without him."

Hand in hand the two girls creep downstairs, open the entrance door carefully and tip-toe out into the lonely, dark courtyard of the Castello.

A Visitor for Bottom

Pitch-black, the castle's two towers stretch towards the dark night sky. Somewhere an owl calls.

Leonie shudders and presses up against Fiona. "Do you have everything?" she asks softly.

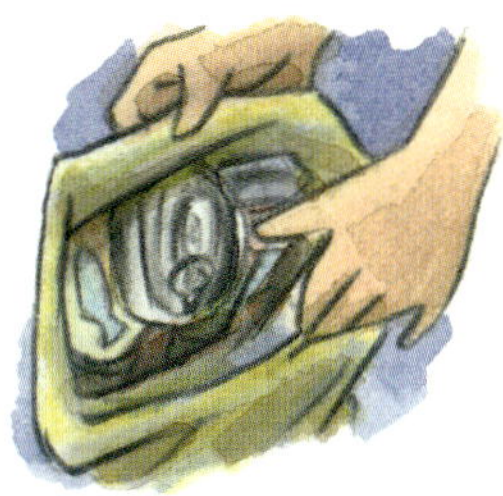

"Tuna, clothes line, torchlight, mask, napkin – everything here. Go and hide behind that bush! I'll sneak over and tie the clothes line to the lantern."

Head bent down, Fiona runs across the courtyard to the broken lantern and ties one end of the clothes line to the post. Then she darts back to Leonie and pulls at the clothes line until it lies flat on the floor and is no longer visible in the darkness.

"Ok. All we need now is Beany," Fiona whispers. "I hope for him he'll turn up!"

She opens the can with the tuna and waves it over her head. But all remains silent. No cat to be heard or seen.

"Beany, you stupid cat!" Fiona scolds

quietly. "Can't you smell the fish?"

"Try one more time," Leonie suggests.

Fiona raises the can again and waves it over her head. A soft breeze moves the branches of the trees. Suddenly, there is a rustling in the bush next to the girls.

"Beany?" Fiona whispers.

Leonie is shaking with fear. A black shadow moves towards the girls.

"About time, you runaway cat!"

Purring loudly, Beany cuddles up to Fiona's leg and begins to eat the tuna at once. While the cat is busy eating, Fiona carefully attaches the mask to his back. Then she points the torchlight at the skull until a greenish glow appears.

"I would never have believed that I'd be so glad to see Filippo's stupid mask. Isn't it great how it glows in the dark like that?"

"That's called fluorescence," Leonie says seriously.

Fiona giggles. “Look, Leonie, now we have a fluorescent cat ghost! I bet the Bottom Crawler has never seen anything quite like that …”

“Shush,” Leonie interrupts Fiona. “I can hear someone coming.”

Fascinated, the two girls are staring through the bush. Two dark figures are walking towards the Castello. One of them is tall and slim, the other one is short and fat. Signore Bottomi and his son are coming.

Hearts beating fast, the friends watch the intruders approach the clothes line. Two more steps to go, one step, half a step …

Fiona holds her breath and watches the two men eagerly. Will everything go well? Yes, it works!

The Bottomis have not noticed the clothes line and are now standing in the middle of the courtyard.

Fiona and Leonie look at each other and nod. Fiona pulls the napkin from her pocket and gives her friend a signal.

"Now," she whispers.

Leonie and Fiona blow hard onto the napkin. It flies up into the air and gracefully descends toward the courtyard. Beany can't be held back any longer!

He leaves the tuna and throws himself into the bush, meowing loudly.

"Bouhouooouuu," howls Fiona. It sounds so spooky it makes her own hair stand on end. "Houhouoouuuu!"

Beany is no longer visible in the darkness.

But the skull mask on his back flashes in one greenish glow across the flagstones, following the napkin. Like a spooky green ghost!

Signore Bottomi and his son scream loudly, turn around and take flight with noisily, clattering steps. Now Fiona and Leonie pull at the clothes line until it is stretched above the ground.

"Aaaaiii," yells the son and flies spectacularly across the clothes line.

"Ouuuuh," cries Signore Bottomi and falls on top of his son.

The clothes line in her hand, Fiona runs toward the two howling men, Leonie hard on her heels. Signore Bottomi is so entangled in the line that he cannot get up. Fiona sits down on the son's fat belly and pins his arms to the ground.

"Ok, all we need to do now is bind them up," Fiona pants and winds the line around the Bottomis' hands and feet.

Leonie checks the knots.

The Bottomis keep on moaning and howling in high voices "Madonna!" and "Maria!".

Suddenly the large squeaky entrance door is opened. Marisa waddles out into the courtyard, a large candle-holder in her hand. Her garish green bathrobe trails behind her in the warm night wind.

"Mamma mia, what is has happened? I have heard the aghastly again! And not only a one aghastly, but two! Madonna! Two aghastlies!"

"No ghosts, Marisa. Only these two clowns here!" Fiona calls out to her and points with her torchlight at Signore Bottomi and his son. "They only wanted to scare you. There are no ghosts here."

"Mamma mia!" Marisa calls out once more, but this time she sounds a lot more cheerful. "No aghastly?"

"No, there is no ghost," Fiona reassures her. "They only wanted you to sell them your castle, so that they can build a hotel here."

"An otel?" Marisa asks in dismay. "And tear down my dear castlo?"

"Who wants to tear down

what?" Now Fabio and Fernando and Filippo have woken up, too, and come down to the courtyard in their blue-white pirate pyjamas.

"Hey, Fiona, could you please explain what this is about?" Filippo has picked up Beany, together with the glowing death mask. A piece of the white napkin is hanging out of Beany's mouth.

"I sure can," Fiona grins.

“Did you actually tie them up?” Fernando asks, pointing at the Bottomis who are still howling, praying and nursing their bruises.

“Hmm, yes,” replies Leonie, “with the clothes line.”

“Fiona, Leonie, is everything alright?” Dad calls from the balcony.

Mum is standing next to him, wearing her flowery nightgown, and looks down into the courtyard in surprise.

Marisa waves at them cheerfully. “Call the police; they can take these criminals here away. And then we can have a big meals with pasta and ham and melon and the rest of the tiramisu!”

"Oh, that's too bad," sighs Leonie. "I'm still so full!"

"There's always room for more food," Fiona decides merrily. "Come on, let's wait for the police. And then we'll have a party."

The Best Holidays Ever

"Oh God, no more food!" Fiona moans, patting her stomach.

It's long past midnight, but nobody wants to go to bed now. All Mamarellas are sitting in their pyjamas and nightgowns in the courtyard, eating and celebrating. Marisa has taken her old record player outside and plays Italian pop songs.

Fiona and Leonie have to recount, again and again, how they have trapped the two Bottomis. And almost every time, Marisa places a new plate full of delicious food in front of Fiona and Leonie, as a reward for their courage. For once, Beany is allowed to play with as many napkins as he likes. Even Fabio, Filippo and Fernando are proud of the girls.

"But this could never ever have worked without my mask," Filippo tells them proudly for about the tenth time. "It could only work with my mask!"

"Alright, alright. Idiot," Fiona grins. Then she turns around to face Leonie, who lies in her chair, looking dreamily up at the stars in the sky. "So, I was right, wasn't I?" Fiona asks.

"Yes, you were", Leonie replies, smiling. "This is the best holiday ever!"

"And you know what the best part of it is?"

Leonie shakes her head and curiously looks at Fiona.

"Well, it's going to last almost another three weeks. Without stupid Bottom-people, and without the aghastly."

"Yeees, that's right, almost three more weeks," Leonie says blissfully.

"And it's not going to be our last holiday at the Castello," Zia Zadora adds, sitting on a little wall next to the bushes, Beany curled up in her lap. Her black eyes glow in the light of the many candles.

Then she bends over towards Fiona and whispers: “Well done, my little mind reader!”

Bettina Belitz was born in Heidelberg in 1973 on a warm summer's day. As a child, she had already begun writing her own stories. After finishing her studies, she worked as a freelance journalist and copywriter. She loves spending her holidays in Italy and lives with her son Mio, her partner and three very stubborn cats together with 400 other inhabitants in a village in the Westerwald.

Alexander Bux, born in Augsburg in 1970, was as a child a passionate painter of monsters and dragons. After school he studied graphic design, focussing on illustration and typography. He has worked in an advertising agency for a few years. Today he lives with his family in Hamburg and enjoys illustrating children's books.

Die nächsten Missionen ...

Fiona ist verzweifelt: Böhnchen, ihr geliebter Kater, ist verschwunden. Und alles deutet darauf hin, dass er entführt wurde! Gemeinsam mit Leonie macht sich Fiona auf die Suche nach dem gemeinen Tierfänger …

Loewe

... warten schon auf Fiona Spiona:

Fionas Papa ist ratlos! Jemand hat versucht, in seine Eisdiele einzubrechen. Aber wer? Und vor allem: warum? Fiona will der Sache auf den Grund gehen und folgt den Spuren des Einbrechers ...

Loewe